THE LIVING WORLD

HOW BIRDS FLY

Nick Williams

W
FRANKLIN WATTS
LONDON•SYDNEY

This edition first published in 2003 by
Franklin Watts
96 Leonard Street
London
EC2A 4XD

Franklin Watts Australia
45-51 Huntley Street
Alexandria
NSW 2015

ISBN: 0 7496 5147 4

A CIP catalogue reference for this book is available
from the British Library.

© Marshall Cavendish Corporation, 1997, 2003

Series created by Discovery Books Ltd.
Originally published as *Nature's Mysteries: How Birds Fly*
by Marshall Cavendish Corporation,
99 White Plains Road, Tarrytown, NY, 10591, USA.

Printed in Malaysia

Acknowledgments
Illustrated by Stuart Lafford (7 top & center, 8–9, 10, 12, 14, 16, 24, 27, 29) and Pat Tourret (7 bottom)
The publishers would like to thank the following for their permission to reproduce photographs: cover Kim
Taylor/Bruce Coleman, title page Kim Taylor/Bruce Coleman, verso Allan G. Potts/Bruce Coleman, 4 Steven C.
Kaufman/Bruce Coleman, 5 William S. Paton/Bruce Coleman, 6 Bruce Davidson/Oxford Scientific Films, 8 Allan G.
Potts/Bruce Coleman, 9 Tony Allen/Oxford Scientific Films, 11 Mik Dakin/Bruce Coleman, 13 top David Tipling/Oxford
Scientific Films, 13 bottom Robert Tyrrell/Oxford Scientific Films, 15 top Gunter Ziesler/Bruce Coleman, 15 bottom
Johnnny Johnson/Bruce Coleman, 17 top Frank Schneidermeyer/Oxford Scientific Films, 17 bottom S. Nielsen/Bruce
Coleman, 18 top S. Nielsen/Bruce Coleman, 18 bottom Hans Reinhard/Bruce Coleman, 19 Kim Taylor/Bruce Coleman
20 Jeff Foott/Bruce Coleman, 20–21 Kim Taylor/Bruce Coleman, 21 Dr Scott Nielsen/Bruce Coleman, 22 left Nick
Williams, 22 right Kim Taylor/Bruce Coleman, 23 Joseph Van Wormer/Bruce Coleman, 25 Gordon Langsbury/Bruce
Coleman, 26 Udo Hirsch/Bruce Coleman, 27 Ben Osborne/Oxford Scientific Films, 28 Gunter Ziesler/Bruce Coleman,
29 top Nick Williams, 29 bottom Wayne Lankinen/Bruce Coleman

(Cover) A young male kestrel taking off.

CONTENTS

MASTERS OF THE AIR

How many times have you seen birds flying in formation high in the sky or flitting among the treetops, looking for food and wished you could fly, too? People have always admired and envied the flying skills of birds and spent hundreds of years trying to copy them. Eventually, we invented the aeroplane, but compared to most birds, the aeroplane is very limited in what it can do.

Since nearly all birds can fly, they can be found just about everywhere — in jungles and deserts, on high mountains, over the oceans, and right in the middle of large cities. Many of them cover huge distances, looking for food or somewhere to breed.

Bald eagles breed mainly in parts of Alaska and Canada far from people and cities. This one is spreading its wide wings as it searches for fish in the water below.

here are more than eight thousand
ifferent species of bird in the world,
nd each flies in a slightly different
ay. We can recognize them in flight
y the way they move and flap their
ings. But why are they able to fly,
id how do they do it?

*Northern gannets are very large sea birds
that nest in large colonies on cliffs and
small islands in the North Atlantic. They
catch fish by diving into the water,
sometimes from great heights. At the last
moment, they close their wings into their
bodies so that they are streamlined as they
hit the water.*

WINGS AND AIRFOILS

Aeroplanes have enough power in their engines to give them lift and thrust for takeoff. Once in the air, the shape of their wings helps to keep them airborne. An aeroplane's wings and tail are fixed, but they have flaps that can change the plane's direction. These flaps are also used in takeoff and landing. Birds can not only change the shape and size of their wings, but they have lots of "flaps" in the form of feathers so they can turn and twist easily.

All birds' wings have some features in common. They are all thicker and rounder at the front and thinner at the back. They are also convex in shape above and concave below. This sort of shape is called an airfoil. The air travels faster as it passes over the top of the wing, so there is less pressure above the wing to push it down.

Underneath, the opposite happens. The air travels more slowly, and there is more pressure to push the wing up. This gives the bird lift.

Large birds, like these pelicans, often fly in V-formation with overlapping wingtips. The bird at the front does the most work, while the others save energy because they do not need to push so hard through the air.

You can see the airfoil shape in this eagle's wing. It helps lift the bird as it flies. This wing shape helps make birds such wonderful flyers.

We copy the shape of a bird's wing when we design aeroplanes. Because they are much heavier than birds, aeroplanes need a long runway to take off, but once they are in the air, they can stay there easily because of the lift they get from their wing shape.

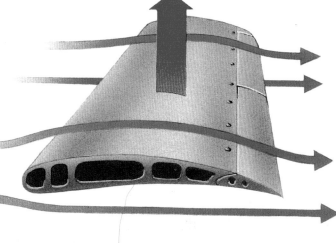

If you hold a piece of paper at one end so that it curves down at the other end, you will have an airfoil shape. When you blow across it, the paper will rise because the pressure of air is stronger below than it is above.

THRUST AND DRAG

As a bird tries to go forward, it's held back by the air pushing against it. This force is called drag. But the shape of a bird is streamlined so that it cuts through the air easily. The more streamlined the bird, the faster it will be.

To achieve the thrust needed to make a bird go forward, the wing rotates and the feathers on the outer part of the wing twist and separate, acting like small propellers to force the air backward and the bird forward.

This shows one complete cycle of a bird's wing beat.

The down stroke gives most of the lift and propulsion.

The up stroke folds the wings and returns them to their original position.

However, it is not just wings that give a bird such control in the air; the tail feathers are important in helping it to twist and turn. When spread out, they also act as a brake just before it lands.

Sooty terns have deeply forked tails, which help them turn easily, and slender bodies and long thin wings, which allow them to fly very quickly. They often fly hundreds of miles in a day, looking for food.

Barn swallows are very agile, using their long wings and tail streamers to quickly twist and turn. They fly low over the ground or water, chasing insects and eating them in flight. They make mud nests in or on artificial objects such as houses, barns, bridges, and mines.

STRONG BUT LIGHT

In order to fly, bird bodies have evolved differently from those of other animals. Over millions of years, weight has been reduced and breathing and circulation have improved.

If we looked inside a bird, we would find that its bones are strong but light. Compared to mammals and reptiles, birds have light jaws and horny beaks that weigh less than teeth. They also have some hollow bones that look like rather a honeycomb on the inside. In addition, some of their bones are fused together. This gives birds a rigid frame without the weight of many large muscles and ligaments.

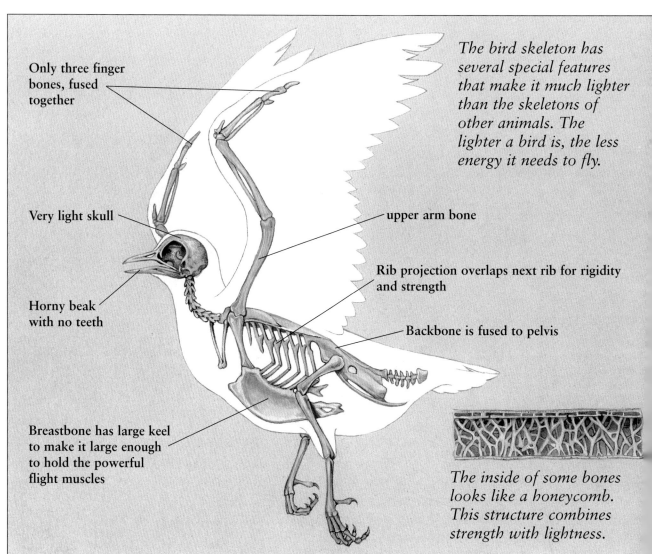

Only three finger bones, fused together

Very light skull

Horny beak with no teeth

Breastbone has large keel to make it large enough to hold the powerful flight muscles

The bird skeleton has several special features that make it much lighter than the skeletons of other animals. The lighter a bird is, the less energy it needs to fly.

upper arm bone

Rib projection overlaps next rib for rigidity and strength

Backbone is fused to pelvis

The inside of some bones looks like a honeycomb. This structure combines strength with lightness.

These light bodies are covered in feathers, remarkable features because they are very strong and very light. (You might have heard the expression "as light as a feather.") They are made from keratin, the same material as reptiles' scales and your hair and nails.

Humans would need chests two metres wide to hold muscles big enough and strong enough to get them into the air! Birds, of course, are much lighter, but they still need large, strong flight muscles.

A bird's breast bone is large and has a keel on it, which gives it stability the same as a keel on a sailing boat.

The muscles that work the wings are joined to the keel, and these muscles have to be very strong. The muscles that pull the wing down are larger than the muscles that push the wings up because more effort is needed to pull the wings down to give the bird lift and propel it through the air. In addition, as the bird lifts its wings up, the wing is folded so there's less surface on it for the air to press upon.

A pigeon needs large chest muscles to get airborne. It takes off by straightening its wings above its back and jumping up far enough to make a down stroke. Then it pulls its wings forward, spreading the feathers to generate lift.

BUILT FOR FLIGHT

Have you ever noticed that the dark meat on a chicken or turkey is around their legs? Because they prefer running around to flying, these birds use their leg muscles far more than their wing muscles, and when you use muscles, you need more oxygen. Oxygen is carried in the blood and this colours the meat red, which makes it dark.

Because flying is so strenuous, birds need a lot of oxygen. They have a special breathing system so they can take in more air. Birds don't just have lungs as we do, but also have lots of air sacs for air storage in their bones. These sacs connect directly to the lungs, which means they can continually use the oxygen they breathe in and can get rid of carbon dioxide gas more easily. In humans (and other animals), the oxygen and carbon dioxide exchange speeds up and slows down, making for a less efficient system. Some birds can even fly as high as the top of Mount Everest in the Himalaya Mountains — where we would need an oxygen mask just to stand on top, since the higher you go, the less oxygen there is.

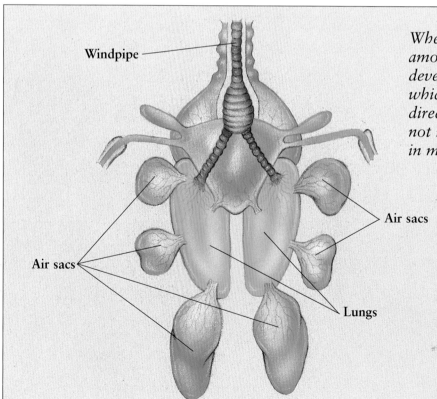

Windpipe

Air sacs

Air sacs

Lungs

When birds fly, they need large amounts of oxygen. They have developed a special system in which air moves in one direction through the lungs, not in and out of the lungs as in mammals.

Birds breathe in air through their windpipe. It is then stored in the inflatable air sacs before flowing through the lungs. Some air sacs are in the bones and breast muscles.

Some birds migrate over high mountains, where there is very little oxygen for them to breathe. These bar-headed geese fly over the Himalaya Mountains twice a year. Like many other birds, they nest in the far north during its short summer and spend the rest of the year much further south, where it is warmer. Very few birds can survive in the Arctic in winter.

rds have large hearts for their size, and ese beat very fast, allowing oxygen to be nt around the body quickly. In some mmingbirds, the heart beats one ousand times per minute, compared to e average human heartbeat of seventy ats per minute.

HOW WINGS WORK

Wings have two main parts. The inner part, which is covered by the secondary feathers, is mainly responsible for giving the bird lift. The outer part, covered by the primary feathers, gives the bird the power to move forward. Lots of birds have general purpose wings, where these two sections are about the same length and the distance from front to back is about half the length.

The shape of a bird's wings depends on the kind of flight they are used for. Pheasants have short wings and large muscles for taking off very quickly to

A bird's wing is made up of several kinds of feathers. Those on the back edge are large and strong, shaped to give lift and help the bird manoeuvre. All the feathers overlap to provide a smooth, streamlined surface.

Coverts are feathers that overlap like roof tiles to make the curved airfoil shape

When a bird opens its wings, the bones are straightened. This extends the wrist and spreads the primary feathers automatically.

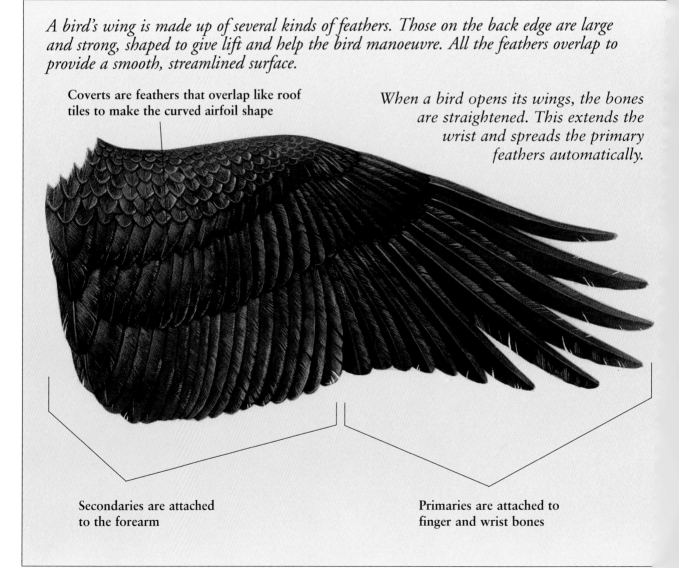

Secondaries are attached to the forearm

Primaries are attached to finger and wrist bones

The Andean condor is the world's largest vulture. It has a wingspan of about three metres and can glide effortlessly.

Power and agility come from having long wings and a light body. Vultures and eagles have long, wide wings for soaring high in the air. Albatrosses have even longer but narrow wings for gliding over the seas and oceans.

...scape from predators, but ...ey can't fly very far. ...irds that need to fly very ...ickly, like falcons and swifts, ...ve long, pointed wings, with a ...uch longer section of primary ...athers to give them power.

The black-browed albatross can fly for months at a time, using air rising from the sea to give it lift.

FEATHER STRUCTURE

All birds have feathers — even penguins, which don't fly. In fact, the way to tell if an animal is really a bird is by its feathers, because no other animal has them. Very small birds, like most hummingbirds, have about one thousand feathers. Swans may have as many as twenty-five thousand, about half of which are on their long necks.

The central stem of the feather is the shaft that grows out of the body. Out of the shaft on either side come rows of barbs, joined together by hundreds of overlapping barbules. These are hooked tightly together by millions of tiny barbicels. This structure makes the feather strong yet flexible.

Feathers on the back edge of the wing and on the tail are very large and strong; they're shaped to form flat, rough, regular surfaces to push against the air. The outer feathers on the body help streamline the shape of the bird.

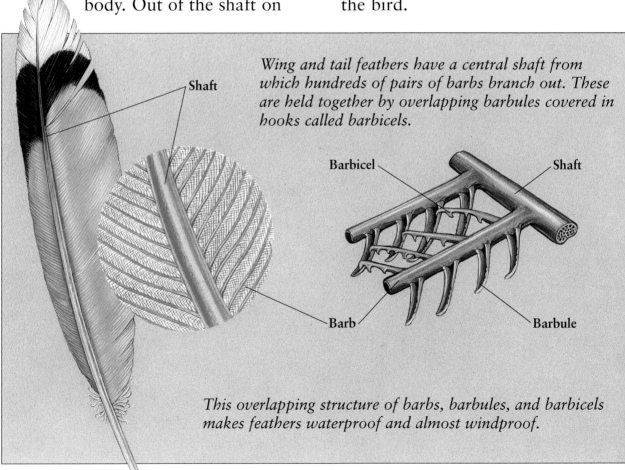

Shaft

Wing and tail feathers have a central shaft from which hundreds of pairs of barbs branch out. These are held together by overlapping barbules covered in hooks called barbicels.

Barbicel

Shaft

Barb

Barbule

This overlapping structure of barbs, barbules, and barbicels makes feathers waterproof and almost windproof.

▲ Feathers are not just for flight. Peacocks, pheasants and birds of paradise all have dazzling, colourful feathers and display them to attract females. The male peacock has very long feathers that normally trail from its back. It raises them in magnificent displays when females are around.

◄ The wing, tail, and other outer body feathers are easy to see, but birds also have an inner layer of downy feathers like those we see on some young birds like ducklings. These feathers help keep them warm.

FEATHER CARE

Birds spend a lot of time caring for their feathers. They clean them, making sure they all fit neatly together and getting rid of parasites, like lice and fleas, that might live on them. This is called preening. Birds use their beaks to do this. They produce a special dust from some of their down feathers and an oily substance from a place just above the base of their tail. They rub this into the feathers to help keep them clean and waterproof.

Some birds, such as these lovebirds, preen each other. Birds that preen themselves have to use their feet to scratch and preen the parts they can't reach with their beaks.

▲ *This preening male mallard is in its eclipse stage, which means that it has molted many of its feathers and is growing new ones. Many male ducks lose their colorful feathers in eclipse and look dull and brown like the females. This helps camouflage them while they are unable to fly.*

However, feathers still become worn and damaged and have to be replaced by new ones. New feathers grow and push the old ones out. This is called moulting.

Different birds moult at different times and in different ways. The feathers of some birds, like the ptarmigan, even change to a different colour for the wintertime. Some birds lose only a few feathers at a time so that they can always fly. Others, like ducks, geese and divers, lose all their flight feathers at once, so they can't fly for three or four weeks. In some species of hornbill, the female loses all her feathers while sitting on her eggs. She is blocked into her nest and fed through a small hole by the male and thus can moult rapidly because she doesn't have to fly out to search for food.

This blue tit is bathing in water to clean its feathers. Many birds also rub themselves in dust to get rid of dirt and lice.

TAKING OFF

Have you ever watched an aeroplane taking off? It zooms along the runway until it reaches flying speed. Large and heavy birds, like swans and flamingos, also need to run before they can take off. They have a wing beat with a lot of lift but little forward speed, so they have to sprint to get going. However, most birds can do so whenever they want to. They may need to take off in a split second to escape from a predator.

Trumpeter swans run across the ice to get up enough speed to take off. They can become so heavy they can't take off any more. Some large birds, such as ostriches and emus, have given up flying altogether and can only escape predators by running away very fast.

These three photographs show a young kestrel taking off from a perch. It leaps off with wings apart and tail feathers lifted and spread out. The kestrel spends many hours each day hovering in the air, looking for small animals on the ground, but if it can find a good perch it can search for food without wasting the energy needed for flying.

Some birds, like pigeons, can take off almost straight up into the air. This uses up a lot of energy, and a pigeon needs to rest for about two minutes before it can take off again. If you disturb one, it will fly right away and then land on something high above the ground, where it is easier to take off.

Albatrosses, with their very long wings, can't take off from the ground on a day when there's no wind. However, if there's a strong wind that they can take off into, they need only a small runway.

Diving ducks, like this ring-necked duck, have legs toward the back of their bodies. They have to run a short distance before taking off. Ducks that don't dive have feet nearer the centre of their bodies, so they can push off better and take off straight up.

LANDING

When landing, birds need to lower their speed to the point where they are just about to stall. This means they push their bodies back, fan out their tails, and flap their wings in such a way that it slows them right down. Small birds have far more control than larger ones. Some can even land upside down on a branch.

▼ *This great black-backed gull is using its tail and wings as brakes to slow it down. As it stalls, it drops down to land on its nest on the cliff edge. Large birds can have great problems trying to land on sea cliffs in a strong wind.*

▲ *This blue tit is about to land upside down on the coconut from below. Small birds like this that feed on branches are very acrobatic and often hang upside down while they eat.*

Canada geese are big birds that need a lot of space to land in because they cannot stop quickly. When they land on water, they push their webbed feet out in front of them to act as brakes and ski along for a short distance before sitting down on the water. These Canada geese are stopping to rest on migration. In winter, they gather in large flocks and migrate south.

However, large birds, like swans and albatrosses, need a long landing strip. It is easier for them to land into a wind, which slows them down, or into water, which helps take the impact of their heavier bodies.

Sometimes, birds need to land quickly. Vultures eat dead animals and they all race to be first to feed on a body. They lower their legs, which act as brakes and increase drag, allowing them to drop rapidly out of the sky.

When they find themselves targets for hunters and predatory birds, geese can lose a lot of height very quickly by rolling to left and right. They can even turn upside down. At the last possible moment, they brake to regain control and land safely.

GLIDING AND SOARING

A glider is an aeroplane without an engine. It is very light and has long wings so that it can glide and soar on the moving air. Gliding for birds means that they can travel through the air without flapping their wings. Some birds, like albatrosses, spend a lot of time gliding.

As land heats up, hot air rises. Air is also sent upward as it hits mountains. Vultures and eagles often live on mountains and in hot places. They soar high into the air and then travel for miles by gliding along on their long, wide wings. This means they can stay in the air for a long time without using energy and getting tired.

Sea birds use the air that rises as it hits cliffs by the sea. They can also glide over the oceans on the air that rises from ships and even on the air that is pushed up by the waves.

▶ *Gannets are large sea birds with a wingspan of more than 1.5 metres. They use the air that rises up the cliffs to fly around their nest sites without using much energy. They also glide over the sea, searching for fish below.*

Air coming from the sea rises when it hits cliffs. This steady current helps sea birds take off and glide effortlessly.

Large birds of prey can soar to great heights, using the currents of hot air that rise from the ground as it heats up.

FLIGHT CONTROL

Birds can change direction quickly by altering the shape of their wings and by pulling with one and pushing with the other. They also use their tails for direction. Fast birds that change direction quickly, like swallows and frigate birds, have long forked tails that give them more control when turning and twisting.

Frigate birds are agile enough to fight in midair, but they mainly use their flying skills to steal food from other birds.

You might have seen a helicopter in the air, not moving up, down, or sideways. This is called hovering. Most birds can hover, even if it's only for a few seconds, but they have to flap their wings very hard and they quickly tire.

Some birds, like ospreys, kingfishers, and terns, often hover over water when they are searching for food, while kestrels hover over open land, looking for mice and other small animals. If the birds hover in still air, when there is no wind, they have to work very hard and they can only do it for a short time. If they use the wind to help them, it makes hovering much easier.

Wilson's storm petrels seem to dance on the water. This one is using its feet to lure small fish to the surface where it can catch them.

The Wing Beat of a Hummingbird

Side view   Top view

The only birds that can hover in still air for a long time are hummingbirds; some can hover without a break for nearly an hour. Their wings move very quickly up to nearly one hundred times a second and the muscles that move the wings are very big for the size of the bird.

LONG DISTANCE FLIGHT

Birds may have to fly a long way to find food, especially in the winter. Some fly thousands of miles at the end of the nesting season, then they fly back again the following spring. This movement is called migration.

Many of the birds that migrate eat flies and other insects, but in colder countries there aren't enough flying insects for them to eat during the winter. Most of them have to fly to warmer places nearer the equator.

Birds with short wings are not made for flying long distances. They have to stop whenever they can to find food. For birds like swifts and swallows, which feed and spend nearly all their time in the air, migration is not so difficult. They simply feed as they fly. Large birds, like storks, use the air currents to glide on when they are migrating, which saves them energy.

Snow geese migrate across North America. They know the route and have favourite places to stop and feed on their journey.

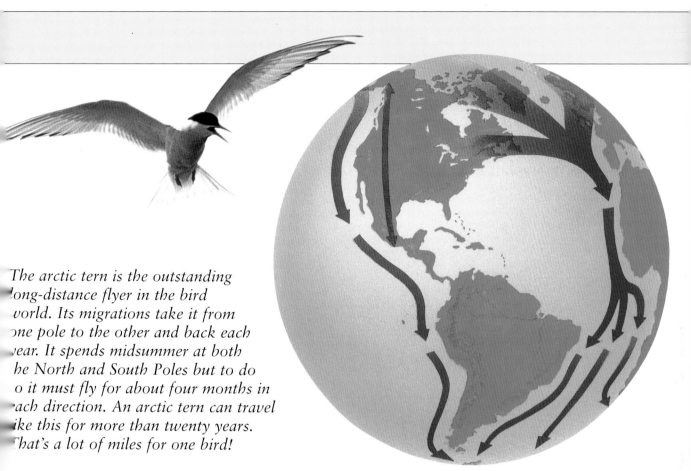

The arctic tern is the outstanding long-distance flyer in the bird world. Its migrations take it from one pole to the other and back each year. It spends midsummer at both the North and South Poles but to do so it must fly for about four months in each direction. An arctic tern can travel like this for more than twenty years. That's a lot of miles for one bird!

→ Rufous hummingbird

→ Arctic tern

Some birds travel enormous distances. Arctic terns fly from where they nest inside the Arctic Circle all the way to Antarctica, and then back again, perhaps flying forty-five thousand kilometres (twenty-eight thousand miles). - the longest flight of any bird. Some birds fly a long way without stopping at all. The lesser golden plover flies without stopping, all the way from Alaska to Hawaii.

But whether birds are built for long distance flight, speed, gliding, or soaring, they will always remain the undisputed masters of the air.

► The rufous hummingbird breeds in the west of America and Canada, and some even reach Alaska. It flies to Mexico every winter – a round trip of 6000 kilometres (3750 miles).

GLOSSARY

camouflage: avoiding being seen by having colours that blend with the background.

circulation: the movement of blood around the body.

concave: having a surface shaped like the inside of a circle.

convex: having a surface shaped like the outside of a circle.

equator: the part of Earth's surface that is an equal distance from both poles.

evolved: developed by a natural process over time.

honeycomb: the structure bees build to store honey in.

keel: the long plate or piece of wood along the bottom of a boat.

ligaments: the flexible tissues that holds bones together.

muscles: bands of tissue that contract to produce movement in animals.

predator: an animal that hunts, kills, and eats other animals.

propellers: revolving shafts with blades, made to drive aeroplanes.

propulsion: the force driving or pushing something along.

species: one sort of bird.

streamlined: shaped to move through the air easily.

USEFUL WEBSITES

To find out more about how birds fly, visit some of the websites listed below. You can also use them to explore other aspects of the living world, and to get involved in nature events across Britain and Australia.

The RSPB website for young people at **www.rspb.org.uk/youth** is the ultimate site for young bird enthusiasts. It is packed with up-to-date information, fun activities and plenty of ideas for getting involved with birding events across Britain and the world!

To find out more about specific birds, visit the Yahooligans' bird web directory at **www.yahooligans.com/content/animals/bird**. You'll find a huge list of birds to choose from, each one accompanied by great photographs and an easy-to-read fact file.

The 'Cool Science for Curious Kids' website at **www.hhmi.org/coolscience** is a fantastic interactive site covering a wide range of science topics.

The Young People's Trust for the Environment is a charity which helps children and young adults explore and understand the environment. The website at **www.yptenc.org.uk** gives up-to-date reports on environmental issues. You will also find lots of ideas on how to get involved in environmental work and events.

Channel 4's excellent educational website provides students and teachers with all the essentials. For help with tricky topics like microorganisms or how things move, visit **www.channel4.com/weblogic/essentials/science/life/index.jsp**

The children's BBC wildlife website, at **www.bbc.co.uk/cbbc/wild,** is a fun and informative site, with easy links to other educational wildlife sites.

To explore Australia's vast and varied natural environment, visit **www.ea.gov.au/education/activities**. This site includes great quizzes, games and activities for children, as well as teaching support materials for teachers.

Note to parents and teachers
Every effort has been made by the Publishers to ensure that these websites are suitable for children; that they are of the highest educational value, and that they contain no inappropriate or offensive material.
However, because of the nature of the Internet, it is impossible to guarantee that the contents of these sites will not be altered. We strongly advise that Internet access is supervised by a responsible adult.

INDEX

Numbers in *italic* indicate pictures